Long-Haired Cats

Jeanne Ramsdale

The breed standards that appear in this book are reprinted from the *CFA Show Standards* booklet and they appear here through the courtesy of the Cat Fanciers' Association, Inc.

© 1984 by T.F.H. Publications, Inc. Ltd.

Distributed in the UNITED STATES by T.F.H. Publications, Inc., 211 West Sylvania Avenue, Neptune City, NJ 07753; in CANADA by H & L Pet Supplies Inc., 27 Kingston Crescent, Kitchener, Ontario N2B 2T6; Rolf C. Hagen Ltd., 3225 Sartelon Street, Montreal 382 Quebec; in ENGLAND by T.F.H. Publications Limited, 4 Kier Park, Ascot, Berkshire SL5 7DS; in AUSTRALIA AND THE SOUTH PACIFIC by T.F.H. (Australia) Pty. Ltd., Box 149, Brookvale 2100 N.S.W., Australia; in NEW ZEALAND by Ross Haines & Son, Ltd., 18 Monmouth Street, Grey Lynn, Auckland 2 New Zealand; in SINGAPORE AND MALAYSIA by MPH Distributors (S) Pte., Ltd., 601 Sims Drive, # 03/07/21, Singapore 1438; in the PHILIPPINES by Bio-Research, 5 Lippay Street, San Lorenzo Village, Makati Rizal; in SOUTH AFRICA by Multipet Pty. Ltd., 30 Turners Avenue, Durban 4001. Published by T.F.H. Publications Inc., Ltd. the British Crown Colony of Hong Kong.

Contents

Introduction 5

Selecting a Longhaired Kitten 6
Pedigree 7
A Healthy Kitten 7
Why Not Two Kittens? 8
Male or Female? 8

Caring for a Longhaired Cat 10
The Litter Box 11
Other Pets in the Household 12
Diet 12
Training 14
Harness and Leash 15
Getting Around With Your Cat 15
Grooming the Longhair 16
Bathing a Longhaired Cat 25
Playthings 28

Your Cat's Health 29
Fleas 29
Hairballs 30
Diarrhea 30
Constipation 31
Fever 31
Parasites 31
Poisoning 32
Skin Troubles 32
Swellings 33
Teeth 33
Feline Urologic Syndrome 33
Rabies 34
Panleukopenia 34
Respiratory Problems 35

Breeding Your Longhaired Cat 36
When to Breed 36
The Expectant Mother 37
Caring for the Mother and Kittens 38

Showing Your Cat 39

Breed Standards 42
Balinese 42
Birman 45
Himalayan 47
Maine Coon 50
Persian 56
Somali 73
Turkish Angora 75

Black and white illustrations
E. Hoy—35
Earl Sherwan—title page

Color photography
Jan Carson—20-21
Robert Pearcy—57
Ron Reagan—60-61

The Persian cat is one of the oldest longhaired breeds.

Introduction

Longhaired cats, according to many fanciers, are the aristocrats of catdom. Their glamorous coats of long fur together with their jewel-like eyes create a living picture of regal beauty. Two of the oldest longhaired breeds are the Persian and the Turkish Angora, and it is believed by some experts that long ago the two breeds may have been crossed in order to establish in the former the silky coat texture of the latter. Through interbreeding with various other cat breeds, the Turkish Angora almost disappeared; in fact, for quite some time the word *angora* was used by people unfamiliar with the cat fancy to describe all sorts of longhaired cats.

Today, however, a variety of purebred longhaired cat breeds can be seen; each exhibits its own unique beauty and elegance, and each is carefully bred according to a particular breed standard of perfection developed by one of the various cat registering associations. To name a few, there are the Balinese (a longhaired Siamese mutation), the Birman (a semi-longhaired breed with Siamese coat color and markings, but with four white paws), the Cymric (pronounced kim-rick, a longhaired Manx—the tailless cat), the Himalayan (a hybrid with Persian type and Siamese markings), the Maine Coon (a large, shaggy-haired breed), the Persian (a round-headed, short-legged, cobby-bodied, natural longhaired breed), the Somali (a semi-longhaired Abyssinian mutation), the Tiffany (a longhaired Burmese mutation), and the Turkish Angora (a natural longhaired breed with a silky-textured coat, as mentioned). Not all of these longhaired breeds are recognized for championship by all cat registering associations.

There are also great numbers of mixed breed longhairs (the result of crossing several breeds) that were bred with no regard to a particular breed standard and whose ancestry is unknown; these animals can be shown in the household pet class provided at most cat shows. In order to be shown, however, mixed breeds must exhibit excellent health and be in top condition.

Selecting A Longhaired Kitten

Cats with long hair should be kept strictly indoors; if they are allowed outside the house, they should be supervised at all times or confined to an outdoor pen. In this way, they cannot get into fights with dogs or with other cats, they cannot be stolen, they avoid the risk of being hit by a car, and they are better able to keep their long, flowing coats clean and untangled. This is not to say that they can manage to groom themselves without their owner's help. All longhaired cats need regular grooming attention, so remember this *before* you make your purchase. In order to keep the cat's beautiful long coat looking its best, you, as a responsible owner, will have to see to it that the animal is brushed, combed, and bathed.

Most longhaired kittens that are for sale, either through pet shops or advertisements, are the products of some cattery. This is a great advantage to the buyer. Nature being what it is, some very unsuitable matches would occur unless breeding was planned. When you purchase a pedigreed kitten, whether you buy its "papers" or not, you have the assurance that a good deal of thought and work have gone into making your kitten what it is. Personality traits, good health, and beauty of form and coat are not accidental. Your cat's pedigree is the record of how all these things have been blended for several (usually three or more) generations.

If you are considering the possibility of breeding and/or showing a longhaired cat, acquaint yourself with its particular breed standard and, if possible, attend a cat show before making your purchase. Then go to a breeder of experience and *good reputation*, and rely on his or her judgment of what is in your best interest.

The difference between a pet-quality and a show-quality

Selecting A Longhaired Kitten

animal is often apparent only to the trained eye. No reputable breeder wants cats from his or her cattery to be shown unless they have the desirable qualities that make them potential winners. Show kittens or cats will of course cost a little more, but they are well worth the extra initial investment if you plan to breed or show them.

Pedigree

Purebred longhaired kittens fall into three general categories: pets, show possibilities, and those with definite show potential. All make equally good pets; however, prices will vary depending on how the breeder classifies the quality of his or her stock. A pedigree, a document which traces a kitten's lineage, is important to have even if you do not plan to show or breed your cat. The animal's ancestry will give you some idea of what to expect from your longhair in terms of its potential disposition and quality. If you do not purchase your cat with a pedigree, be sure to get a statement from the breeder, preferably in writing, as to whether the pedigree and other important papers (registration, health certificate, and so on) will be available at a later time and at what cost. Keep in mind that a cat without proof of pedigree may not be purebred. With pet-quality longhairs, most breeders will furnish the necessary documents only after the animal has been altered (males are neutered and females are spayed).

A Healthy Kitten

Be sure the kitten you choose is alert, with bright and clear eyes. It should be well fleshed, with a substantial feel. These are characteristics of the healthy cat. Steer clear of a kitten with a runny nose, sore ears, skin lesions, or a drab-looking, harsh-feeling coat. It is a wise precaution to have the kitten you choose checked by a veterinarian who can determine the animal's condition. A "bargain price" animal can cost a great deal more in disappointment and veterinary care than one purchased at a

Selecting A Longhaired Kitten

higher price. Wait a while, and save your money for the *right* longhaired cat if you cannot afford to buy it now.

Most longhaired kittens should be at least ten weeks of age before they are taken to a new home. The extra weeks with its mother, after weaning, provide the animal with a much better start in life. The kitten has also had time to get its vaccinations and to build immunity to some of the common cat diseases which are dangerous and nearly always fatal. The kitten's digestive processes have developed sufficiently by this age so that changes in environment, food, and water will not make it sick. A cat that is properly weaned is usually socialized and its individual personality pattern is present. In addition, its mother has had time to teach it the ways of life, such as how to groom its coat and how to use the litter box.

Why Not Two Kittens?

One kitten is fun—two kittens are more fun. Often a family finds that one kitten does not "go around" so they return to purchase another. A single cat very often gets spoiled. When you have two, they have cat companionship and competition, and they develop playing routines that defy description! If the kittens are of different sexes, plan to have them altered. And be careful not to bring up a brother and sister together unless you prevent them from breeding.

Male or Female?

Although males and females make equally good pets, each sex has different personality characteristics. Keep in mind, however, that even though there are differences between the sexes, each cat has its own individual disposition. Try to choose one that suits you. The males are usually larger and more boisterous. The females are usually more delicately built and "girlish" in their behavior. Both are equally lovable in their own special ways. Unspayed females are potential mothers whether you wish it or not. Having a

Selecting A Longhaired Kitten

male neutered is less expensive and not a serious operation, nor does it cause him to grow fat and lazy, as is so often claimed.

An altered cat of either sex makes a better pet than one subject to the periodic sexual urges of nature. Cats are rather intense about their love life and seem to suffer emotionally if prevented from pursuing it. When they are altered, all of this energy is diverted in other directions. They become more relaxed, playful, and loving. The recommended age for altering a male is approximately seven or eight months, before any serious hormone activity gets started. A female cat can come into season (heat) and become pregnant at any time after approximately five months of age, although the first season usually occurs at about seven or eight months. The age at which a longhaired cat matures sexually varies from breed to breed and from individual to individual. Your veterinarian can guide you in this matter. Spaying should be done early if there is any possibility of a female getting together with any male. Altered cats may be entered in cat shows to compete only against others of the same status.

After you have chosen your kitten, or it has chosen you, be prepared to enjoy development from babyhood through adolescence, to full flower as an adult. Again, depending on the breed, females generally mature to their full beauty at about two to three years. Males of four or five years of age are at their peak. The older a cat becomes, the more personality, intelligence, and beauty it seems to possess, so that your ownership is a continuing pleasure.

Caring for a Longhaired Cat

Most longhaired cats that are kept as pets share their living space with their owners inside the home. But cattery cats may be kept in large enclosures in special sections of the home or they may live in their own "houses" outside. Mine live in or out depending on the circumstances. There are many satisfactory types of housing construction for an outdoor cattery; those that are most appropriate take into consideration the cat's basic requirements of comfort and protection. Whenever screen wire is used, for example, be certain to fasten a heavier-gauge wire mesh (such as hardware cloth) to the framework interior. The reason for this is because cats have the tendency to rip through thin layers of wire screen. Avoid using rough wire, such as chicken wire, if you plan to construct an outdoor cattery, because the fur of a longhaired cat can easily get caught in this. A solid-roofed, solid-walled permanent structure will provide protection from the elements; however, a screened-in porch or run can be attached to the structure so that in nice weather the cats can sun themselves and exercise in the fresh air. A door or portal can be installed so that the cats can enter the screened-in enclosure.

Cattery accommodations can vary depending on your time, money, ingenuity, and the space and resources available. A typical walk-in enclosure might look something like this: A set of sturdy, glass-paned double doors (screened in summer) provide easy access to the cats' living quarters. Adequate lighting and ventilation are provided, and temperature control is carefully monitored. Sturdy carpeted shelves on which the residents can perch are fastened to the interior walls. Several windows strategically positioned provide fresh air, sunshine, and offer the cats a view of their surroundings. The entire structure is insulated; it is heated in winter, cooled in summer, draft-free, and it is set up on a concrete foundation (or concrete blocks). The interior walls and floor are constructed of linoleum, a material that can be easily cleaned. Sleeping accommodations are provided for

Caring for a Longhaired Cat

each cat, and food, water, and litter boxes are easily accessible. There is outdoor plumbing (hot and cold running water) to make cleaning chores easier. Built-in counter tops and cabinets offer storage space for supplies. A small refrigerator keeps opened cans and packages of food from spoiling.

Another type of outdoor cattery (not a walk-in model) might feature three stories, each of which is divided into large compartments. Trap doors between each floor allow room for the cats to exercise, as they jump from one level to another. Panels that separate each compartment are removable so that various accommodations can be provided for the tenants. Other structural features are similar to the walk-in house already described, including the concrete foundation, solid roof and walls, proper ventilation, and so on. A tarpaulin or canopy can be fastened to the structure to provide extra protection during inclement weather, and a screened-in porch can be added.

The Litter Box

A litter box, a fairly deep pan filled with any one of several brands of commercial litter, is essential for your kitten. I have found litter to be the most satisfactory material, and the deodorizing and superabsorbent qualities well justify the cost. You might want to first line the bottom of the litter box with some sheets of newspaper or plastic (to help make cleaning the pan easier) or you may want to purchase litter pan liners for the same purpose. Then add the litter. Newspaper alone, sand, or dirt are not suitable litter materials: they may be cheap, but in the long run they just do not do the job. I recommend putting the litter box in a sturdy cardboard carton with high sides or on an island of newspapers, because cats often make a great project of "covering up" and fling the litter out of the pan for some distance. If the cardboard box is too high for the kitten to jump into, cut an entry hole in one side. If you have a very large home, it would be wise to have a second "bathroom" set up for

Caring for a Longhaired Cat

your pet. A very young kitten might not be able to reach one litter box in time, since it will put off the necessary trip until the last minute; if the animal has another box nearby, chances are accidents will be avoided. Kittens are usually cooperative about using the litter box and only fail to do so when ill, frightened, or confused about its location. If your kitten is trained to one material and you wish to change to a different type, do it gradually. Put a little of the new material in with the old, gradually increasing the amount each day until the old type is entirely eliminated.

After each meal, place the kitten in its litter and it will be housebroken very quickly. You can dispose of the used litter promptly so that there will be no unpleasant cat odor about the house.

Other Pets in the Household

Most cats get along with and like, or at least tolerate, most dogs or other pets. It is best to introduce strangers to one another gradually by sight and smell and always be with them at first. By the time the new pet has acquired a familiar "house smell," you can leave it alone with another animal if no violent hostility has manifested itself. There may be a good deal of jealousy at first. You can help in this situation by giving extra attention and reassurance to the jealous one, who will then blame *you* more than the interloper for the change in its household.

Diet

If possible, feed your newly acquired cat or kitten what it has been used to eating. Change the diet gradually to avoid digestive upsets. Quite often a cat in new surroundings is not too interested in food. Exploration comes first! Do not be alarmed if this is the case. Try later with fresh food—a healthy animal will soon be hungry.

A young kitten should be fed small quantities often, perhaps four or five times a day. They eat a little, play, sleep, and then eat a little more. Kittens from

Caring for a Longhaired Cat

four to eight months old can be fed on a more regular, three-meal-a-day basis. A kitten's growth pattern is variable, so adjust the amount of food to its appetite. The adult cat needs only morning and evening feedings. Naturally a pregnant female or nursing mother requires more food and extra calcium. Check with your veterinarian about this.

Individual requirements and tastes govern the amount of food served at any one time and the frequency of meals. A cat may eat more in the evening, some eating from time to time during the entire night. Some cats have a reputation for being fussy eaters. They will relish a certain type or brand of food one day and refuse it the next. On the other hand, some cats want only fish, liver, kidney or whatever happens to be their particular fancy. Fortunately, many different kinds of cat foods have become available, so that any cat's taste should be satisfied.

A varied, well-balanced diet is very important for health and beauty. A proper cat diet requires a high proportion of protein, fats, and fatty acids. A cat also needs more vitamin B, B-12, and B-complex than any other animal. To see that your cat is provided with these and all the other necessary elements, keep in mind what a cat would eat if it were free to select its own menu. In the wild, fish, birds, and other vegetable- and grain-eaters such as rabbits and mice are eaten nearly whole. So it follows that meat with fat, organ meats, cereal, bone meal, vegetables, dairy products, fish, and eggs all have a place in your cat's diet. Some cats have loose bowels from drinking milk; if this is the case, other dairy products can be substituted. Raw liver in quantity also can have an effect on the bowels; but since it is such a valuable vitamin source, try to include a small amount of it from time to time mixed with the regular food.

Access to some fresh greens (you may want to sprout your own) is desirable; not only do they supply valuable minerals, but they serve as an emetic as well. Nibbling on greens helps the cat purge hairballs that may have formed in its stomach or

Caring for a Longhaired Cat

intestines as a result of its licking the fur and, in so doing, swallowing the hair. Meat should be cut into bite-size pieces that will require chewing. Be sure to remove all meat from the bone: avoid giving your cat bones that will splinter when chewed and that will be swallowed easily. Dry foods are nutritious and good for jaw development; these hard morsels are especially effective in preventing tartar from forming on the cat's teeth.

Vitamin supplements will eliminate any possibility of deficiency in the diet. They also give added support through the cat's different stages of growth. There are liquid products that can be given with an eye dropper and powdered ones that can be sprinkled on the cat's food.

Fresh water should be available to your kitten or cat at all times. The water and food dishes should be washed with soap and hot water and rinsed well each day.

Training

Kittens and cats can be easily toilet trained; however, training them to do or not to do other things is more difficult. A very good way of training a cat to come to you whenever you want it to is always to whistle for it at mealtime. Rather shrill notes seem to get the best action and are readily heard, even outdoors. Your cat will also learn its name if addressed with it, rather than being called "kitty."

A cat seems to be impressed by noise and commotion. Sharp clapping of hands and loud noises with a paper will at least make the animal pause in the course of wrongdoing. Try to make it appear as if the interesting, forbidden object—such as the bird, furniture, rug, or door—is itself attacking the cat with noise. Your cat will learn the meaning of No even if it doesn't always wish to admit it. It will respond to praise and love and, in general, will want to please you. You'll soon realize that your pet is like a small child—it will do anything to get your attention, even actions it knows will be frowned upon. The cat will also misbehave to express its

Caring for a Longhaired Cat

displeasure at your actions—such as leaving it alone!

If you set up a scratching post, and teach your cat how to use it, you will take the cat's mind and claws off the furniture and rugs. Kittens often pretend that scratching posts are real trees and do some fancy tricks on them. Claw clippers made especially for cats can be used to good advantage, particularly to curb the tendency of a young kitten to climb on and scratch everything.

Harness and Leash

A cat can be trained to a harness and leash. A collar is not recommended because it can rub the fur off the ruff of a longhaired cat and cause matting and bare spots beneath. It's also easy for the cat to pull its head out of a collar. The best harness is a figure eight style. This can be easily worn by the cat, and it fastens on top so that hair doesn't get caught in the buckle. It will be almost impossible for your pet to choke on or pull out of this type of arrangement. One loop forms an oval around the head and shoulders and the other goes under the belly toward the back. With a soft leather or nylon-web harness, there is little friction on the fur.

A young cat will consider a leash just something to play with. At first the youngster will often act as though it can't walk or stand up with a harness on. This phase passes with practice. The harness and leash can be used when the animal is outdoors, provided your yard is protected from visiting cats, dogs, and children who might harm and have the advantage over a pet tied to a leash. Be careful to tie the leash where it cannot get wound around anything.

Getting Around With Your Cat

Whenever you take your cat out of the house or yard, it should be in a carrier or on a leash. There are several reasons why this is desirable and important. Since the cat is not used to the outside world,

15

Caring for a Longhaired Cat

sudden noises or movements can startle and frighten it, resulting in its escape or your getting scratched or bitten. Riding in the car can be made easier for both of you. If the animal is in a transparent carrier or one with a window, you can set the cat up high enough to see out if it wants to. By using a carrier, your pet does not get bounced around and you do not have to watch out for it underfoot or when windows and doors are opened. You can cover the carrier wholly or partially if you have to leave the cat alone in the car so that "catnappers" won't be tempted. Also, when the carrier is used on a trip to the veterinarian, it may prevent your cat from being exposed to other cats' diseases or from curious strange dogs. The carrier, if left open in the house, becomes a familiar place of refuge when the animal is exposed to unsettling experiences.

A cat carrier for longhaired cats should be well-ventilated with room inside for a small litter box. Pet shops stock various sturdy carriers in a variety of shapes, sizes, and prices; you are sure to find one that will suit your cat's needs.

Grooming the Longhair

Even when your kitten is so young that combing is not strictly needed, it is good to have a daily stint with the brush and comb. This gets you and the kitten into the grooming habit. The comb should be made of steel with long slim teeth to get all the way through the fur to the skin. First use a comb with wide-set teeth to straighten out the tangles and break up large accumulations of knotted fur. Then switch to a finer-toothed

---

Captions for color photos:
Odd-eyed white Persian kitten, page 17. Longhair with plume-like tail, page 18. Red and white bi-color longhair; this cat is not a Persian, page 19. Arden's Manitou of Schick, a red mackerel tabby Maine Coon. Breeder, Carol Knowles. Owner, Sharyn and Richard Bass, pages 20-21. Playing with a bit of yarn, page 22. Longhair scratching itself with its hind leg. This cat is probably pestered by fleas, page 23. Tabby longhair head study, page 24.

Caring for a Longhaired Cat

comb to pick up loose fur and get out the small knots which can otherwise build up to matted spots. Get a very fine-toothed comb for removing fleas (if there are any) and also to use on the shorter face fur. Some combs are available with two teeth sizes.

Pay particular attention to the flanks (the sides), the pants (the back of the hind legs), inside both the front and hind legs, the tummy, under the chin and chest, and behind the ears. These are the potential trouble spots, especially when the cat's undercoat begins to shed. Some people unknowingly just comb the back, head, and tail and find, to their sorrow, that the underside has become felted into a solid mattress of fur. This condition requires the scissors or a trip to the veterinarian.

After combing, brush against the grain of the fur to stimulate growth and to bring out the glossiness of the cat. Fur around the ruff (the neck) should be combed and brushed up and out to form an Elizabethan collar, or frame, for the face. A natural-bristle brush causes less static electricity and hair breakage than a brush made of nylon bristles.

If your cat's ears are oily, clean them gently with a cotton swab as often as necessary. Gently wipe away matter that may have collected in and around the eyes.

Regular grooming of a longhaired cat is very important. This way there will be fewer hairs around the house; and even during shedding seasons, your cat will maintain its health and beauty with fewer hairballs to be ingested and less chance of sore skin due to knots and matting.

Bathing A Longhaired Cat

If you comb and brush your longhaired cat every day, there will be little need to bathe it. I have found the powder shampoos and cleaners very helpful for spot cleaning. Cornstarch or talcum powder also can be used. In places where it is difficult for a cat to wash itself—behind and in front of the ears, under the chin, and down the bib—the fur is apt to get a little oily or greasy. Simply part the fur and shake powder in it. Brush down to the skin and out until the soil is

Caring for a Longhaired Cat

absorbed. Repeat the application of powder, if necessary, until each hair stands separately. Put your hand loosely over the cat's face to shield its eyes and nose from the powder as you are working. There are also liquid solutions for cleaning the fur and these are best applied with a soft brush or cotton. Foam cleaners do not seem to be suited for use on longhaired cats.

If your cat has gotten so dirty that a soap and water bath is the only solution, try to enlist the aid of another person. An extra hand or two at the right time can be very helpful. First assemble all the things you will use for the bath, including two or three large towels. There are many good cat shampoos and cleaners on the market. Consult a pet store owner for a brand they recommend. With longhaired cats there is a great variation in coat texture and soilability; some cats are neat and always look spotless, whereas others attract dirt the way some children do!

Before bathing your cat, comb it thoroughly and clean inside the ears with wet, then dry, cotton swabs. Put a drop of mineral oil in each eye to lessen possible soap irritation.

Now fill the sink or tub halfway with warm water before you place the cat in it. Or you can wet the cat with a spray attachment, and fill the tub with only enough water standing to soak the cats feet. Wetting the cat is the first problem, because the fur sheds water and it is so thick that it takes time to get the cat wet to the skin. A spoonful of mild liquid detergent in the water makes it "wetter," and enables it to soak into the coat more readily.

When the cat is wet, start working the shampoo in gradually to the skin. Do the head first. The fleas—if there are any—will congregate there and can be seen easily in the short face fur. A washcloth is helpful in cleaning around the head and face. The skin in front of the ear openings sometimes gets oily and should be scrubbed well. Used gently, an old toothbrush is good for this purpose.

Next, check the skin around the tail. This spot may need special attention. Often there is a brownish, oily substance known

Caring for a Longhaired Cat

as "stud oil" exuded around the base and top ridge of the tail. This is less common in females than males, but it can be present in either sex. When this is not removed, it not only discolors and separates the fur but also forms a crust on the skin which causes sores and baldness in this area. If this is a continual problem, the *tail only* can be scrubbed with a toothbrush and detergent shampoo as often as necessary to prevent oil accumulation. Damp boric acid packs also help control this condition. After you have prewashed the tail, shampoo the cat all over and work the lather down to the skin. Rinse the cat thoroughly with a spray as long as necessary to remove *all* traces of soap. Finish with a very diluted solution of white vinegar, or with a cream rinse (which helps remove tangles) followed by another clear water rinse.

If your cat should happen to get into paint, grease, tar, or oil, soak the affected parts with salad oil or olive soil. Squeeze out the oil and repeat the procedure (using clean oil each time until it comes clear.) Follow this with a soap and water bath.

Wring out the wet fur by squeezing it to the cat's body, particularly the fur covering the legs and feet. Wrap the cat in one towel and dry its face with another. This boosts the animal's morale, which may be low at this point, especially if this is its first bathing experience. Rough-dry the rest of the coat with a dry towel, as long as the cat will permit it. You can then use whatever you have in the way of a drying facility, provided the air is not too hot or cold. A hair dryer set on a low setting, the blower end of a vacuum cleaner, or a combination of oven and fan might work, although not all cats will accept these methods, so you will have to experiment. No matter what method you use, it is important to dry the cat as quickly and safely as possible. Keep the animal out of drafts so that it does not catch cold as its fur dries. If it is a warm, sunny day, you might want to let the cat dry naturally outside (in an enclosed area of course). As the cat dries, be careful that it does not get too hot with the sun on its topside. The underside and

Caring for a Longhaired Cat

back legs take the longest to get dry unless the animal stands up and moves around. The natural tendency of a wet cat, however, seems to be to huddle down as flat as possible.

There is no danger in giving a soap and water bath to a healthy cat. The danger lies in not getting the cat completely bone dry *to the skin*, and in the subsequent possibility of lowered resistance due to chilling. Hold the fur to your face for a few minutes to detect the least trace of dampness.

If you plan to show your cat, it must be spotless. A soap and water bath or its equivalent is a must. However, experiment beforehand to learn how many days it takes after bathing for the coat to look its best. Govern your pre-show bath accordingly. Too frequent bathing of any cat dries out the skin and dulls the luster of the fur. Bathing several days in advance of a show gives the natural oils in the cat's coat time to come to the surface and give the coat a nice glow.

It is rather an ordeal for a longhaired cat to be bathed so remember to offer lots of praise regarding its beauty and good behavior. Give the cat something tasty to eat and let it take a nice long nap after its bath session.

Playthings

Toys, especially ones that make a little noise, are enjoyed by young and old cats. Cardboard houses with many doors and windows can be a source of great amusement for both you and your cat. Something like this can be made from a large carton, or you can purchase a very elegant playhouse at most shops.

Your Cat's Health

When a cat or kitten shows little interest in food or has diarrhea for more than a day, it needs attention. Cats generally are very healthy, so if they don't seem to exhibit "normal" behavior, there must be some reason for it. Lack of appetite and/or loose bowels is symptomatic of nearly all cat ailments. Although sometimes the reason is simple, prompt treatment is important. Amateur diagnosis can be harmful, expensive, and may cost your cat's life. If the animal does not respond quickly to the suggested remedies for minor ailments, consult your veterinarian immediately. In good faith and ignorance, you can do more harm by treating the cat yourself, since so many illnesses are closely related or have similar symptoms. The cheapest life insurance for your pet is availing yourself of a veterinarian's experienced skill *promptly* if anything seems abnormal.

Many of the following problems can be avoided by keeping your cat inside where you can observe its actions and eliminate its exposure to disease.

Fleas

Fleas are a common problem and are very detrimental to a cat's health and beauty. Scratching the itching flea bites ruins the coat and causes matting, and fleas may be carriers of the tapeworm, an internal parasite. Getting rid of tapeworms after you have eradicated the fleas is a job for the veterinarian. Evidence of fleas are grains of "flea dirt" on the cat's skin and throughout the coat. This is a black substance, gritty to the touch, which turns red when wet. With persistent effort you can completely eliminate fleas on your cat; it helps to keep the animal inside. Even though you think you may have eradicated the problem, keep in mind that flea eggs drop off the cat; the larvae hatch in various places around the house, then enter a pupa stage, and later emerge as adult fleas and jump back aboard the cat.

So, not only does the cat need to be treated for fleas, but its environment needs attention as well.

Wash all washable articles, and

Your Cat's Health

vacuum often, particularly in dark corners and crevices of the room. Sprinkle flea powder on and under rugs and furniture cushions. Be sure you use a preparation made especially for cats. There are several (liquids, powders, and sprays) that are very effective yet nontoxic to cats. A small amount of flea-killing preparation placed on the base of the cat's tail and on the back of its neck, applied daily for ten days to two weeks, should rid your cat of fleas. In addition, you will have to thoroughly clean the animal's surroundings (carpeting, furniture, the cat's bed, to name but a few places) in order to help control the problem.

Hairballs

The more thoroughly you brush and comb your cat to remove dead hair, the fewer hairs will be ingested by the animal as it grooms itself. Cats swallow the loose hairs that shed when they lick themselves. These hairs accumulate in the animal's digestive tract where they form wads, and many cats will vomit them or pass them in their bowel movements. If they do, there is no problem. To make sure that they pass, give your cat a weekly dosage of one of the various hairball remedies that are commercially available. Some of these preparations are packaged in tubes; simply squeeze out a small amount and allow the cat to lick it off. This lubricant will facilitate the passage of hairballs as they occur. *Never* administer liquid lubricants (such as salad oil or mineral oil) orally, as the cat could possibly inhale this into its lungs. In extreme cases, hairballs may have to be surgically removed, although regular brushing and combing of the cat's fur together with the administration of hairball preparations should suffice in most instances.

Diarrhea

Simple digestive upsets, evidenced by loose bowels and/or vomiting, can be treated with remedies such as Kaopectate®. A teaspoonful (less for a kitten) given three to four times a day

Your Cat's Health

should relieve these symptoms. If they persist, call your veterinarian. Diarrhea is often a symptom of any one of several ailments, although it is often related to diet.

Constipation

Difficult or infrequent bowel movements suggest the need for a change in diet: check with your veterinarian about this. He or she will probably recommend high fiber foods and dietary lubricants, both of which will help loosen the stool so that it can be easily passed. As mentioned in the section on hairballs, *never* administer liquid lubricants orally.

Fever

A cat's normal body temperature is 101 to 102°, and it is best taken rectally. If you do not have a thermometer, you can detect a fever by holding your hand across the cat's ears and face. This area will feel extremely warm if a fever is present. The cat's pawpads also will feel quite warm to the touch. Excitement can cause fever, although a rise in temperature usually indicates an infection of some kind and as such requires treatment by a veterinarian. Occasionally, when a kitten is cutting its permanent teeth from three to seven months of age, it will run a high temperature as well as lose its appetite because of sore gums. Check with your veterinarian about what medication to offer that will return the cat's temperature to normal.

Parasites

General poor condition, a lusterless coat, bare patches in the fur (from itching, scratching, and biting), weight loss even though the appetite is good, chronic loose bowels, and, in some cases, an allergic eczema reaction, can each—or all—be symptoms of parasitic infection.

Tapeworm segments, similar in appearance to grains of rice, are eliminated in the cat's stool and can be detected there, or they

Your Cat's Health

can be seen clinging to the hairs around the anus. Since fleas are intermediate hosts of tapeworms, it is doubly important to keep your cat and its surroundings free of them. Roundworms also may be passed in the cat's stool or they maybe vomitted up. The presence of worms can be determined by your veterinarian who will want to analyze a sample of the cat's stool. When the vet has determined what worms, if any, are present, he will then suggest a method of treatment.

Ear mites themselves are not apparent to the naked eye. The irritation of the ear canal, caused by their presence, produces a brown or black crumbly wax in and about the ears. Scratching the ears and shaking the head are indications of a possible infestation. Ear mites are extremely contagious among cats and other animals. Persistent treatment with an effective product recommended by your veterinarian can easily clear up the condition once it is discovered.

Poisoning

Many chemicals are poisonous to cats. Particularly dangerous are DDT, Chlorodane, and Lindane in any form, as well as arsenic and coal tar derivatives such as preparations containing carbolic acid. If you suspect poisoning, call your veterinarian at once. Bring along the container of poison if possible; this will facilitate treatment since the antidote can be more quickly determined. As a cat owner, you must make certain to keep poisonous household products far from kitty's reach.

Skin Troubles

The skin of some cats breaks out due to allergies. Because ringworm and other fungal diseases can also cause this, it is vital that an expert diagnosis be made so that proper treatment can be undertaken as soon as possible. New methods, using drugs that work internally, have shown great promise for speedily eradicating ringworm. Treatment is a very lengthy problem on a

Your Cat's Health

longhaired cat if the condition does not receive *immediate* attention.

Swellings

Swelling on any part of the body indicates injury and/or infection. A cat's skin heals very readily; thus, a scratch or bite wound will seal over on top, outwardly showing no break, but infection can be running rampant beneath and throughout the system. Treatment, after lancing and antibiotic injections, consists mainly of keeping the scab removed so the wound can heal from the inside out.

Teeth

Your cat's teeth should be checked periodically for tartar accumulations. When tartar is present, the teeth should be scaled (by your veterinarian) to prevent irritation of the gums and opportunity for infection. Infected teeth should be removed. Dry foods help keep the gums and teeth in good condition, so these hard morsels should be part of the cat's diet and made available at all times.

Feline Urologic Syndrome

There are several symptoms involved with regard to this disorder and they can be seen individually or in combination. Some cats may develop an inflammation of the bladder (cystitis), while others may develop sand-like particles which then lie in the urinary tract (urolithiasis). When these sand-like particles form plugs or stones, the urine either cannot be passed easily or it cannot be passed at all (urethral blockage). When a cat cannot urinate, due to an obstruction, poisonous wastes begin to accumulate in the bloodstream (uremia). If the obstruction is not removed immediately, a swift death can result. Although both males and females can be affected by FUS, males are particularly susceptible to blockage due to the small size of the urethra.

If your cat makes frequent trips to its litter box and strains

Your Cat's Health

to urinate or defecate with few or no results, notify your veterinarian at once. Often this straining is misinterpreted by the cat owner as constipation. Failure to use the litter box (using instead the sink or bathtub, for example) and/or evidence of blood in the urine are signs to watch for.

Rabies

Check with your veterinarian about having your cat inoculated against rabies; all warm-blooded animals (man included) are susceptible to this viral disease and domestic cats are no exception. The disease is transmissible through the saliva of a rabid animal, and such mammals as skunks, raccoons, bats, and foxes are often carriers of the rabies virus. Your cat may contract the disease if it is bitten or scratched by a rabid animal or if it comes in contact with the animal's contaminated saliva. This is a good reason why your cat should not be allowed to roam out-of-doors, especially if you live near a wooded area where many of these potential carriers of rabies may live. Animals with "dumb" rabies may seem lethargic and may exhibit signs of paralysis; often a drooping jaw is seen. "Furious" rabies indicates a more aggressive behavior, with frequent attacks of vicious biting and scratching. Since there is no cure for rabies, the best form of prevention of this dreadful disease is with the appropriate vaccination.

Panleukopenia

Also known as feline distemper, feline infectious enteritis, and cat fever, among other names, this highly contagious disease can affect cats of all ages, particularly young kittens. Mention should be made here that there is no connection of this feline disease with canine distemper. Kittens should be vaccinated at approximately eight to nine weeks of age, and booster shots should be given as further protection every year or so, as recommended by your veterinarian. Onset of the disease is characterized by weakness,

Your Cat's Health

The Himalayan is basically a Persian cat with Siamese markings.

fever, depression, loss of appetite, vomiting of a yellowish fluid, diarrhea (which may also be yellowish or bloody), dehydration, weight loss, and hanging of the head over the water dish. The course to death is often so swift that the disease is mistaken for poisoning. All cats, regardless of age, should be vaccinated against this contagious disease.

Respiratory Problems

Symptoms of such feline respiratory infections as rhinotracheitis, calicivirus, and pneumonitis are similar to the human cold or flu. Watery eyes, runny nose, sore throat, coughing, sneezing, and body aches are commonly seen. The cat may be feverish, listless, and it may lack its normal appetite; sometimes the bowels are loose. Vaccinations, often given in conjunction with the one for panleukopenia, are a necessary precaution, followed by regular booster shots throughout the cat's life. If your cat does become ill and shows signs of respiratory infection, the individual should be isolated, particularly in catteries or in households where there are many feline residents, so as not to infect the other animals. Your veterinarian can prescribe an effective treatment.

Breeding Your Longhaired Cat

Cat breeding is a specialized field: do not undertake it without careful consideration of what would be involved in the way of time, effort, money, and appropriate facilities for the care and sale of the prospective family. If you *do* want to care for a litter of kittens, then maintain close contact with an experienced breeder and with a veterinarian through all of the phases of reproduction to prevent costly errors.

When to Breed

If you own a female cat, a breeder can help you select the best possible mate (stud) for her and this person can give you valuable advice about what desirable traits this mate may carry in its bloodline. The mating should be planned and arranged well in advance of the actual breeding time. Female cats have regular estrous cycles throughout the year, and within each cycle are several periods during which the female can be bred. These periods of "coming into season" or of "being in heat" occur every few weeks and last for approximately three to seven days. The frequency and duration of these periods vary considerably, depending on the individual cat and its particular breed. A fertile female can conceive at any time during these periods of heat. Even if she has already been bred, she is capable of mating again during the same period. The unfortunate result is kittens that may be sired by more than one father. This is why it is vitally important to confine an impregnated queen who has just mated with a stud of your own choosing. Make certain that the queen does not come into contact with another sexually mature tom. Do not let her out of the house.

In most cases the female is brought to the male, and it is a good idea to put the two prospective parents together at the first signs of heat in the female. She will begin to call with rather loud and persistent vocalizations, and she will roll on the ground and generally become restless. After being transported to strange surroundings, your female may feel apprehensive at

Breeding Your Longhaired Cat

first about mating; but after settling down in a day or two, she should become receptive to the idea. Often breeders will leave the male and female together for a period of time just to make certain the mating was successful. If it was, the female's estrous cycle will be arrested until after the kittens are born.

The Expectant Mother

The kittens are carried inside their mother for about nine weeks. If you have the mother examined by a veterinarian about three to four weeks after breeding, he can usually determine how many kittens she is carrying. This will prove to be valuable information at the time of delivery. Litter size varies depending on the particular breed and the individual cat. The veterinarian will also advise you of any diet change or supplements that might be needed.

Closets are highly favored spots for having kittens. In advance of the event, prepare a large cardboard box or bed lined with a small blanket. A pet cat will usually insist on you, or someone, being with her constantly before and during the delivery process.

If the mother is in hard labor for several hours without results, she may need assistance. Do not delay asking for expert help from the veterinarian; prompt care can save the youngsters' lives. Delivery can be difficult for some breeds, such as Persians, because kittens can be large-boned and too big for the mother to give birth to without assistance.

The kittens are born in an amniotic, fluid-filled, sac. An inexperienced mother sometimes does not realize the necessity of removing the filmy membrane from the kitten's mouth and nose after birth, so it can breathe. Do this yourself, *immediately*, if she doesn't. Severing the umbilical cord from the placenta is of less urgency, but it should also be done by you if the mother fails to do this.

Breeding Your Longhaired Cat

Caring for the Mother and Kittens

Once the kittens have arrived and are breathing properly and getting nourishment from their mother, usually there are few problems. Kittens are born blind; the eyes open at a week to ten days of age. Keep the kittens in a dark place until their eyesight is fully developed, then gradually expose them to an increasing amount of light. If the eyelids stick back together after opening, bathe the eyes with cotton soaked in a mild boric acid solution (one teaspoon to eight ounces of water), or use warm water. If the condition persists, use an eye ointment recommended by your veterinarian.

Check the kittens often during the first few days to see that they are being fed. They should feel fully packed and rounded within twenty-four hours after birth. If you have to hand-feed them, use one of the commercial formulas available in most pet shops, (Esbilac or KMR, for instance) and administer it with an eyedropper or a plastic doll bottle. Frequency of feeding depends on age and intake, on the basis of two- to four-hour intervals. But be sure to check with your veterinarian first before you attempt to hand-feed the youngsters.

Ordinarily the mother will care for all of the kittens' needs until they are old enough, at about four weeks, to climb out of the box. From this time on they gradually start to eat, lap milk, and go to the litter box at their mother's direction, with little assistance from you. Weaning usually is complete by six to eight weeks of age. The mother can come in season again anytime shortly after having kittens, so guard against accidental breeding. Only one litter a year is advised, unless in certain cases the female can become more run-down by constant calling than by having another family. The drain on the mother cat's system is heaviest when she is nursing, and she should be watched for signs of calcium deficiency particularly around the time the kittens are three to four weeks old and if the litter is large.

You'll probably hate to part with

Showing Your Cat

any of the kittens, but a houseful of mischievous young animals may be too much for you to handle. You should have no trouble finding good homes for the litter. Your pet shop owner may be interested in buying a kitten. Word of mouth is usually the best advertisement, and friends who know that your cat has had kittens will tell others. Don't be surprised if you find strangers on your doorsteps, eager for a kitten of their own. A notice placed on the bulletin board of your neighborhood supermarket may also be used to good advantage in selling kittens, and an ad in your local newspaper is a tried and true method. Be certain to find good homes for the kits, to ensure they will receive proper love and care.

A cat's formal, or registered, name tells a good deal about it. A cattery prefix, which indicates the animal's breeder, usually proceeds the call name (the name by which the animal is referred or called); sometimes a cattery suffix is added to the cat's name if the animal is subsequently owned by another cattery. Most cat registering associations limit the number of letters in a registered cat's name (including all three parts—the prefix, the call name, and the suffix). To illustrate, Dearheart Terry of Donegai was bred at Dearheart Cattery but now belongs to Donegai Cattery. The animal's call name is, of course, Terry.

There are several national organizations for the purpose of registering the names and pedigrees of purebred cats. These organizations also sanction shows and keep records of the wins made at the cat shows, which are staged by their affiliated clubs. The rules and procedures of each national organization differ slightly but are very similar in many respects. A cat may attain championship and grand

Showing Your Cat

championship status in any one association, or in several associations. This accounts for the double, triple, etc., champion title preceding a show cat's name. Quint. Ch. Beverly-Serrano Roger of Dearheart is an example of a five-time winner with five different registering associations.

To briefly summarize show procedure, your entry form is solicited and returned by you to the entry clerk approximately one month prior to the date of the show. Entries are recorded and cataloged according to breed, color, sex, and the various classes. In the nonchampionship classes are kittens (four to eight months of age), altered cats and household pets. Championship classes are divided into novice, open, champion and grand champion divisions. The novice class is only for those cats over eight months of age and, in some associations, under two years, who have not yet won a first place, or blue, ribbon. The open class includes all cats who have not won the required number of points to claim their championships. Champion and grand champion classes, respectively, are for those who have achieved that status. Winners of the novice and open class of each sex compete for "winner's points," or points toward championship, in each breed and color. Those receiving these points then compete against the champion and grand champion first-place winners for best male, or female, of their color. Best of color and best of color opposite sex are selected from these two. Divisional bests are chosen from these best of colors and opposites. Then, in all-breed shows, best and opposite longhair, best and opposite shorthair, and finally best, second best, best opposite sex, and second best opposite sex in show are chosen. There are also wins given for best and best opposite sex of each class—novice, open, championship, etc., as well as for each of the nonchampionship groups. Usually a longhair and a shorthair specialty show is benched in conjunction with an all-breed show, with their own separate judges choosing their "bests" in each of the above

Showing Your Cat

categories also.

When you arrive at the show as an exhibitor, your cat is assigned to a display cage provided by the show management. You furnish the interior of the cage to your own taste so that it will best show off your exhibit. Litter and food are usually provided for your cat to use. Your cat is listed and numbered in the official catalog but is judged by the number only. Judging cages are in a separate area and unmarked. The cat's number is placed on top of the judging cage and indicates the order in which it is to be brought to the judging area. The cat is placed in the cage from the rear, and the judge removes the animal from the front. Shows are open to the general public and usually admission is charged. Further information about clubs and local shows can be obtained by writing to the secretaries of the various national cat registering organizations. Following is a list of organizations that register cats and that sanction cat shows.

American Cat Association (ACA)
American Cat Fanciers' Association (ACFA)
Canadian Cat Association
Cat Fanciers' Association (CFA)
Cat Fanciers' Federation (CFF)
Crown Cat Fanciers' Federation (CROWN)
The International Cat Association (TICA)
United Cat Federation (UCF)

Since the Cat Fanciers' Association, Inc. is the largest and one of the oldest cat registering bodies, we have included several of their breed standards (for longhaired breeds) to give readers an idea of what breeders strive for in their cats, and what judges look for as they evaluate those entries in the show ring. Each cat registering association develops its own set of standards, one for each of the breeds it recognizes for championship. A Balinese standard, for example, is an *ideal*; it describes what the perfect Balinese cat should look like. The closer a Balinese show cat comes to conforming to its breed

Breed Standards

standard, the more likely it is to win. Longhaired mixed breeds, or household pets, are not judged against purebred longhairs; instead, they are judged on their beauty and condition. There are no standards used in household pet competition.

Purebred longhaired cats, in this case a Persian, are bred according to a breed standard of perfection.

BALINESE

Point Score

HEAD (20)
    Long Flat Profile.......... 6
    Wedge, fine muzzle, size.... 5
    Ears 4
    Chin................... 3
    Width between eyes........ 2

EYES (5)
    Shape, size, slant,.......... 5
    and placement

BODY (30)
    Structure and size,........ 12
    including neck
    Muscle tone.............. 10
    Legs and Feet............. 5
    Tail.................... 3

COAT (20)
    Length 10
    Texture 10

COLOR (25)
    Body Color.............. 10
    Point Color.............. 10
    (matching points of dense color, proper foot pads and nose leather)
    Eye Color................ 5

GENERAL: The ideal Balinese is a svelte, dainty cat with long

Breed Standards

tapering lines, very lithe but strong and muscular. Excellent physical condition. Neither flabby nor boney. Not fat. Eyes clear. Because of the longer fur the Balinese appears to have softer lines and less extreme type than other breeds of cats with similar type.

HEAD: long, tapering wedge. Medium size in good proportion to body. The total wedge starts at the nose and flares out in straight lines to the tips of the ears forming a triangle, with no break at the whiskers. No less than the width of an eye between the eyes. When the whiskers and face hair are smoothed back, the underlying bone structure is apparent. Allowance must be made for jowls in the stud cat.

SKULL: Flat. In profile, a long straight line is seen from the top of the head to the tip of the nose. No bulge over the eyes. No dip in nose.

NOSE: Long and straight. A continuation of the forehead with no break.

MUZZLE: Fine, wedge-shaped.

CHIN AND JAW: Medium size. Tip of chin lines up with tip of nose in the same vertical plane. Neither receding nor excessively massive.

EARS: Strikingly large, pointed, wide at base, continuing the lines of the wedge.

EYES: Almond shaped. Medium size. Neither protruding nor recessed. Slanted towards the nose in harmony with lines of wedge and ears. Uncrossed.

BODY: Medium size. Dainty, long, and svelte. A distinctive combination of fine bones and firm muscles. Shoulders and hips continue same sleek lines of tubular body. Hips never wider than shoulders. Abdomen tight. The male may be somewhat larger than the female.

NECK: Long and slender.

LEGS: Long and slim. Hind legs higher than front. In good proportion to body.

Breed Standards

PAWS: Dainty, small, and oval. Toes, five in front and four behind.

TAIL: Bone structure long, thin, tapering to a fine point. Tail hair spreads out like a plume.

COAT: Long, fine, and silky without downy undercoat.

COLOR: *Body:* Even, with subtle shading when allowed. Allowance should be made for darker color in older cats as Balinese generally darken with age, but there must be definite contrast between body color and points. *Points:* Mask, ears, legs, feet, tail dense and clearly defined. All of the same shade. Mask covers entire face including whisker pads and is connected to ears by tracings. Mask should not extend over top of head. No ticking or white hairs in points.

PENALIZE: Lack of pigment in the nose leather and/or paw pads in part or in total. Crossed eyes.

DISQUALIFY: Any evidence of illness or poor health. Weak hind legs. Mouth breathing due to nasal obstruction or poor occlusion. Emaciation. Kink in tail. Eyes other than blue. White toes and/or feet. Incorrect number of toes. Definite double coat (i.e., downy undercoat).

Balinese Colors

SEAL POINT: Body even pale fawn to cream, warm in tone, shading gradually into lighter color on the stomach and chest. Points deep seal brown. *Nose Leather and Paw Pads:* Same color as points. *Eye Color:* Deep vivid blue.

CHOCOLATE POINT: Body ivory with no shading. Points milk-chocolate color, warm in tone. *Nose Leather and Paw Pads:* Cinnamon-Pink. *Eye Color:* Deep vivid blue.

BLUE POINT: Body bluish white, cold in tone, shading gradually to white on stomach and chest. Points deep blue. *Nose Leather and Paw Pads:* Slate-colored. *Eye Color:* Deep vivid blue.

Breed Standards

LILAC POINT: Body glacial white with no shading. Points frosty grey with pinkish tone. *Nose Leather and Paw Pads:* Lavender-Pink. *Eye Color:* Deep vivid blue.

BIRMAN
(Sacred Cat of Burma)

Point Score

HEAD 30
(including size and shape of eyes, ear shape and set)

TYPE 25
(including shape, size, bone, and length of tail)

COAT 10

COLOR 25

EYE COLOR 10

HEAD: Skull strong, broad, and rounded. Forehead slopes back and is slightly convex. There is a slight flat spot just in front of the ears.

NOSE: Roman in shape, nostrils set low. Length in proportion to size of head.

CHEEKS: Full. The fur is short in appearance about the face, but to the extreme outer area of the cheek the fur is longer.

JAWS: Heavy.

CHIN: Full and well-developed. Lower lip is strong, forming perpendicular lines with upper lip.

EARS: Medium in length. Almost as wide at the base as tall. Modified to a rounded point at the tip; set as much to the side as into the top of the head.

EYES: Almost round.

BODY: Long but stocky.

LEGS: Medium in length and heavy.

PAWS: Large, round, and firm. Five toes in front, four behind.

TAIL: Medium in length, in pleasing proportion to the body.

COAT: Long, silken in texture,

Breed Standards

with heavy ruff around the neck, slightly curly on stomach. This fur is of such a texture that it does not mat.

COLOR: *Body:* Even, with subtle shading when allowed. Strong contrast between body color and points. *Points Except Paws:* Mask, ears, legs, and tail dense and clearly defined, all of the same shade. Mask covers entire face including whisker pads and is connected to ears by tracings. No ticking or white hair in points. *Front Paws:* Front paws have white gloves ending in an even line across the paw at the third joint. *Back Paws:* White glove covers the entire paw and must end in a point, called the laces, that goes up the back of the hock.

PAW PADS: Pink preferred, but dark spot on toe/pad acceptable because of the two colors in pattern.

EYES: Blue in color. The deeper blue the better. Almost round in shape.

PENALIZE: White that does not run across the front paws in an even line. Siamese type head. White shading on stomach and chest.

DISQUALIFY: Lack of white gloves on any paw. Kinked or abnormal tail. Crossed eyes. Incorrect number of toes. Areas of pure white in the points, except paws.

Birman Colors

SEAL POINT: Body even pale fawn to cream, warm in tone, shading gradually to lighter color on the stomach and chest. Points, except for gloves, deep seal brown. Gloves pure white. *Nose Leather:* Same color as the points. *Paw Pads:* Pink. *Eye Color:* Blue, the deeper and more violet the better.

BLUE POINT: Body bluish white, cold in tone, shading gradually to almost white on stomach and chest. Points, except for gloves, deep blue. Gloves pure white. *Nose Leather:* Slate-color. *Paw Pads:* Pink. *Eye Color:* Blue, the deeper and more violet the better.

Breed Standards

CHOCOLATE POINT: Body ivory with no shading. Points, except for gloves, milk-chocolate color, warm in tone. Gloves pure white. *Nose Leather:* Cinnamon-Pink. *Paw Pads:* Pink. *Eye Color:* Blue, the deeper and more violet the better.

LILAC POINT: Body a cold, glacial tone verging on white with no shading. Points, except for gloves, frosty grey with pinkish tone. Gloves pure white. *Nose Leather:* Lavender-Pink. *Paw Pads:* Pink. *Eye Color:* Blue, the deeper and more violet the better.

HIMALAYAN

Point Score

HEAD 30
 (including size and shape of ears, ear shape and set)

TYPE 20
 (including shape, size, bone, and length of tail)

COAT 10

BODY COLOR 10

POINT COLOR 10

EYE COLOR 10

BALANCE 5

REFINEMENT 5

HEAD: Round and massive, with great breadth of skull. Round face with round underlying bone structure. Well set on a short, thick neck.

NOSE: Short, snub, and broad. With "Break."

CHEEKS: Full.

JAWS: Broad and powerful.

CHIN: Full and well developed.

EARS: Small, round tipped, tilted forward, and not unduly open at the base. Set far apart and low on the head fitting into (without distorting) the rounded contour of the head.

EYES: Large, round, and full. Set far apart and brilliant, giving a sweet expression to the face.

Breed Standards

BODY: Of cobby type—low on the legs, deep in the chest, equally massive across shoulders and rump, with a short well-rounded middle piece. Large or medium in size. Quality the determining consideration rather than size.

BACK: Level.

LEGS: Short, thick, and strong. Forelegs straight.

PAWS: Large, round, and firm. Toes carried close, five in front and four behind.

TAIL: Short, but in proportion to body length. Carried without a curve and at an angle lower than the back.

COAT: Long and thick, standing off from the body. Of fine texture, glossy and full of life. Long all over the body, including the shoulders. The ruff immense and continuing in a deep frill between the front legs. Ear and toe tufts long. Brush very full.

COLOR: *Body:* Even, free of barring, with subtle shading when allowed. Allowance to be made for darker coloring on older cats. Shading should be subtle with definite contrast between points. *Points:* Mask, ears, legs, feet, tail dense and clearly defined. All of the same shade, and free of barring except for Lynx-Points. Mask covers entire face including whisker pads and is connected to ears by tracings. Mask should not extend over top of head. No ticking or white hairs in points.

PENALIZE: Lack of pigment in nose leather and/or paw pads in part or in total. Any resemblance to Peke-Face Persian.

DISQUALIFY: Locket or button. Any tail abnormality. Crossed eyes. Incorrect number of toes. White toes. Eyes other than blue.* Apparent weakness in hind quarters. Deformity of skull and/or mouth.

*Editor's Note: "Eyes other than blue" applies to Himalayans that are not solid-colored.

Breed Standards

Himalayan Colors

SEAL POINT: Body even pale fawn to cream, warm in tone, shading gradually into lighter color on the stomach and chest. Points deep seal brown. *Nose Leather and Paw Pads:* Same color as points. *Eye Color:* Deep vivid blue.

CHOCOLATE POINT: Body ivory with no shading. Points milk-chocolate color, warm in tone. *Nose Leather and Paw Pads:* Cinnamon Pink. *Eye Color:* Deep vivid blue.

BLUE POINT: Body bluish white, cold in tone, shading gradually to white on stomach and chest. Points blue. *Nose Leather and Paw Pads:* Slate-colored. *Eye Color:* Deep vivid blue.

LILAC POINT: Body glacial white with no shading. Points frosty grey with pinkish tone. *Nose Leather and Paw Pads:* Lavender-Pink. *Eye Color:* Deep vivid blue.

FLAME (RED) POINT: Body creamy white. Points deep orange flame to deep red. *Nose Leather and Paw Pads:* Flesh or Coral Pink. *Eye Color:* Deep vivid blue.

CREAM POINT: Body creamy white with no shading. Points buff cream with no apricot. *Nose Leather and Paw Pads:* Flesh Pink or Salmon Coral. *Eye Color:* Deep vivid blue.

TORTIE POINT: Body creamy white or pale fawn. Points seal with unbrindled patches of red and cream. Blaze of red or cream on face is desirable. *Nose Leather and Paw Pads:* Seal brown with flesh and/or coral pink mottling to conform with colors of points. *Eye Color:* Deep vivid blue.

BLUE-CREAM POINT: Body bluish white or creamy white, shading gradually to white on the stomach and chest. Points blue with patches of cream. *Nose Leather and Paw Pads:* Slate blue, pink, or a combination of slate blue and pink. *Eye Color:* Deep vivid blue.

SEAL LYNX-POINT: Points

Breed Standards

beige-brown ticked with darker brown tabby markings. Body color pale cream to fawn, warm in tone. Mask must be clearly lined with dark stripes vertical on forehead with classic *M* on forehead, horizontal on cheeks and dark spots on whisker pads clearly outlined in dark color edges. Inner ear light with thumbprint on outer ear. Markings dense, clearly defined and broad. Legs evenly barred with bracelets. Tail barred. No striping or mottling on body, but consideration to be given to shading in older cats. *Nose Leather:* Seal or Brick Red. *Paw Pads:* Seal. *Eye Color:* Deep vivid blue.

BLUE LYNX-POINT: Points light, silvery blue, ticked with darker blue tabby markings. Body color bluish white, cold in tone. Mask must be clearly lined with dark stripes vertical on forehead with classic *M* on forehead, horizontal on cheeks and dark spots on whisker pads clearly outlined in dark color edges. Inner ear light with thumbprint on outer ear. Markings dense, clearly defined and broad. Legs evenly barred with bracelets. Tail barred. No striping or mottling on body, but consideration to be given to shading in older cats. *Nose Leather:* Blue or Brick Red. *Paw Pads:* Blue. *Eye Color:* Deep vivid blue.

CHOCOLATE SOLID COLOR: Rich, warm chocolate-brown, sound from roots to tip of fur. *Nose Leather and Paw Pads:* Brown. *Eye Color:* Brilliant Copper.

LILAC SOLID COLOR: Rich, warm lavender with a pinkish tone, sound and even throughout. *Nose Leather and Paw Pads:* Pink. *Eye Color:* Brilliant Copper.

Allowable outcross breeds - Persian.

MAINE COON

Point Score

HEAD (30)
    Shape 15
    Ears 10

Breed Standards

Eyes 5

BODY (35)
Shape 20
Neck 5
Legs and Feet 5
Tail 5

COAT (20)

COLOR (15)
Body Color 10
Eye Color 5

GENERAL: Originally a working cat, the Maine Coon is solid, rugged, and can endure a harsh climate. A distinctive characteristic is its smooth, shaggy coat. With an essentially amiable disposition, it has adapted to varied environments.

HEAD SHAPE: Medium in width and medium long in length with a squareness to the muzzle. Allowance should be made for broadening in older studs. Cheek bones high. Chin firm and in line with nose and upper lip. Nose medium long in length; slight concavity when viewed in profile.

EARS: Large, well-tufted, wide at base, tapering to appear pointed. Set high and well apart.

EYES: Large, wide set. Slightly oblique setting.

NECK: Medium long.

BODY SHAPE: Muscular, broad-chested. Size medium to large. Females may be smaller than males. The body should be long with all parts in proportion to create a rectangular appearance. Allowance should be made for slow maturation.

LEGS AND FEET: Legs substantial, wide set, of medium length, and in proportion to the body. Paws large, round, well-tufted. Five toes in front; four in back.

TAIL: Long, wide at base, and tapering. Fur long and flowing.

COAT: Heavy and shaggy; shorter on the shoulders and longer on the stomach and britches. Frontal ruff desirable. Texture silky with coat falling smoothly.

Breed Standards

PENALIZE: A coat that is short or overall even.

DISQUALIFY: Delicate bone structure. Undershot chin. Crossed eyes. Kinked tail. Incorrect number of toes. Buttons, lockets, or spots.

Maine Coon Colors

EYE COLOR: Eye color should be shades of green, gold, or copper, though white cats may also be either blue or odd-eyed. There is no relationship between eye color and coat color.

Solid Color Class

WHITE: Pure glistening white. *Nose Leather and Paw Pads:* Pink.

BLACK: Dense coal black, sound from roots to tip of fur. Free from any tinge of rust on tips or smoke undercoat. *Nose Leather:* Black. *Paw Pads:* Black or Brown.

BLUE: One level tone from nose to tip of tail. Sound to the roots. *Nose Leather and Paw Pads:* Blue.

RED: Deep, rich, clear, brilliant red; without shading, markings, or ticking. Lips and chin the same color as coat. *Nose Leather and Paw Pads:* Brick Red.

CREAM: One level shade of buff cream, without markings. Sound to the roots. *Nose Leather and Paw Pads:* Pink.

Tabby Color Class

CLASSIC TABBY PATTERN: Markings dense, clearly defined and broad. Legs evenly barred with bracelets coming up to meet the body markings. Tail evenly ringed. Several unbroken necklaces on neck and upper chest, the more the better. Frown marks on forehead form an intricate letter *M*. Unbroken line runs back from outer corner of eye. Swirls on cheeks. Vertical lines over back of head extend to shoulder markings which are in the shape of a butterfly with both upper and lower wings distinctly outlined and marked with dots inside outline. Back

Breed Standards

markings consist of a vertical line down the spine from butterfly to tail with a vertical stripe paralleling it on each side, the three stripes well separated by stripes of the ground color. Large solid blotch on each side to be encircled by one or more unbroken rings. Side markings should be the same on both sides. Double vertical row of buttons on chest and stomach.

MACKEREL TABBY PATTERN: Markings dense, clearly defined and all narrow pencillings. Legs evenly barred with narrow bracelets coming up to meet the body markings. Tail barred. Necklaces on neck and chest distinct, like so many chains. Head barred with an *M* on the forehead. Unbroken lines running back from the eyes. Lines running down the head to meet the shoulders. Spine lines run together to form a narrow saddle. Narrow pencillings run around the body.

SILVER TABBY: Ground color pale, clear silver. Markings dense black. White trim around lip and chin allowed. *Nose Leather:* Brick Red desirable. *Paw Pads:* Black desirable.

RED TABBY: Ground color red. Markings deep, rich red. White trim around lip and chin allowed. *Nose Leather and Paw Pads:* Brick Red desirable.

BROWN TABBY: Ground color brilliant coppery brown. Markings dense black. Back of leg black from paw to heel. White trim around lip and chin allowed. *Nose Leather and Paw Pads:* Black or Brown desirable.

BLUE TABBY: Ground color pale bluish ivory. Markings a very deep blue affording a good contrast with ground color. Warm fawn overtones or patina over the whole. White trim around lip and chin allowed. *Nose Leather:* Old Rose desirable. *Paw Pads:* Rose desirable.

CREAM TABBY: Ground color very pale cream. Markings of buff or cream sufficiently darker than the ground color to afford good contrast but remaining within the dilute range. White

Breed Standards

trim around lip and chin allowed. *Nose Leather and Paw Pads:* Pink desirable.

CAMEO TABBY: Ground color off-white. Markings red. White trim around lip and chin allowed. *Nose Leather and Paw Pads:* Rose desirable.

PATCHED TABBY PATTERN: A Patched Tabby (Torbie) is an established silver, brown, or blue tabby with patches of red and/or cream.

Tabby With White Class

TABBY WITH WHITE: Color as defined for Tabby with or without white on the face. Must have white on bib, belly, and all four paws. White on one-third of body is desirable. Colors accepted are Silver, Red, Brown, Blue, or Cream.

PATCHED TABBY WITH WHITE (Torbie with White): Color as described for Patched Tabby (Torbie) but with distribution of white markings as described in Tabby with White. Color as described for Patched Tabby (Torbie) with or without white on face. Must have white on bib, belly, and all four paws. White on one-third of body desirable. Colors accepted are Silver, Brown, or Blue.

Parti-Color Class

TORTOISESHELL: Black with unbrindled patches of red and cream. Patches clearly defined and well broken on both body and extremities. Blaze of red or cream on face is desirable.

TORTOISESHELL WITH WHITE: Color as defined for Tortoiseshell with or without white on the face. Must have white on bib, belly, and all four paws. White on one-third of body is desirable.

CALICO: White with unbrindled patches of black and red. White predominant on underparts.

DILUTE CALICO: White with unbrindled patches of blue and cream. White predominant on underparts.

Breed Standards

BLUE-CREAM: Blue with patches of solid cream. Patches clearly defined and well broken on both body and extremities.

BLUE-CREAM WITH WHITE: Color as defined for Blue-Cream with or without white on the face. Must have white on bib, belly, and all four paws. White on one-third of the body is desirable.

BI-COLOR: A combination of a solid color with white. The colored areas predominate with the white portions being located on the face, chest, belly, legs, and feet. Colors accepted are Red, Black, Blue, or Cream.

Other Maine Coon Colors Class

CHINCHILLA: Undercoat pure white. Coat on back, flanks, head, and tail sufficiently tipped with black to give the characteristic sparkling silver appearance. Legs may be slightly shaded with tipping. Chin, ear tufts, stomach, and chest pure white. Rims of eyes, lips, and nose outlined with black. *Nose Leather:* Brick Red. *Paw Pads:* Black.

SHADED SILVER: Undercoat white with a mantle of black tipping shading down from sides, face, and tail from dark on the ridge to white on the chin, chest, stomach, and under the tail. Legs to be the same tone as the face. The general effect to be much darker than a Chinchilla. Rims of eyes, lips, and nose outlined with black. *Nose Leather:* Brick Red. *Paw Pads:* Black.

SHELL CAMEO (RED CHINCHILLA): Undercoat white, the coat on the back, flanks, head, and tail to be sufficiently tipped with red to give the characteristic sparkling appearance. Face and legs may be very slightly shaded with tipping. Chin, ear tufts, stomach, and chest white. *Nose Leather, Rims of Eyes, and Paw Pads:* Rose.

SHADED CAMEO (RED SHADED): Undercoat white with a mantle of red tipping shading down the sides, face, and tail from dark on the ridge to white on the chin, chest, stomach, and under the tail. Legs to be the same tone as face. The general effect to be much redder than the Shell Cameo. *Nose Leather, Rims of Eyes, and Paw*

Breed Standards

Pads: Rose.

BLACK SMOKE: White undercoat, deeply tipped with black. Cat in repose appears black. In motion the white undercoat is clearly apparent. Points and mask black with narrow band of white at base of hairs next to skin which may be seen only when fur is parted. Light silver frill and ear tufts. *Nose Leather and Paw Pads:* Black.

BLUE SMOKE: White undercoat, deeply tipped with blue. Cat in repose appears blue. In motion the white undercoat is clearly apparent. Points and mask blue with narrow band of white hairs next to skin which may be seen only when fur is parted. White frill and ear tufts. *Nose Leather and Paw Pads:* Blue.

CAMEO SMOKE (RED SMOKE): White undercoat, deeply tipped with red. Cat in repose appears red. In motion the white undercoat is clearly apparent. Points and mask red with narrow band of white at base of hairs next to skin which may be seen only when fur is parted. *Nose Leather, Rims of Eyes, and Paw Pads:* Rose.

Allowable outcross breeds -None.

PERSIAN

Point Score

HEAD 30
 (including size and shape of eyes, ear shape and set)

TYPE 20
 (including shape, size, bone, and length of tail)

Captions for color photos:
Supreme Grand Champion Friscoon's Buffalo Bill, a brown tabby with white male and winner of numerous awards. Bred and owned by Pat Herrmann and Robert Salerno, page 57. Black and white bi-color longhair, page 58. A Persian cat keeps its Terrier friend company, page 59. Pair of Maine Coon cats in their own special hideaway, pages 60-61. Tabby longhair yawning, page 62. Blue-point Himalayan, page 63. Tabby Longhair, page 64.

Breed Standards

COAT 10

BALANCE 5

REFINEMENT 5

COLOR 20

EYE COLOR............... 10

In all Tabby varieties, the 20 points for color are to be divided 10 for markings and 10 for color.

HEAD: Round and massive, with great breadth of skull. Round face with round underlying bone structure. Well set on a short, thick neck.

EARS: Small, round tipped, tilted forward, and not unduly open at the base. Set far apart, and low on the head, fitting into (without distorting) the rounded contour of the head.

EYES: Large, round, and full. Set far apart and brilliant, giving a sweet expression to the face.

NOSE: Short, snub, and broad. With "Break."

CHEEKS: Full

JAWS: Broad and powerful.

CHIN: Full and well developed.

BODY: Of cobby type, low on the legs, deep in the chest, equally massive across shoulders and rump, with a short well-rounded middle piece. Large or medium in size. Quality the determining consideration rather than size.

BACK: Level.

LEGS: Short, thick, and strong. Forelegs straight.

PAWS: Large, round, and firm. Toes carried close, five in front and four behind.

TAIL: Short, but in proportion to body length. Carried without a curve and at an angle lower than the back.

COAT: Long and thick, standing off from the body. Of fine texture, glossy and full of life. Long all over the body, including

Breed Standards

the shoulders. The ruff immense and continuing in a deep frill between the front legs. Ear and toe tufts long. Brush very full.

DISQUALIFY: Locket or button. Kinked or abnormal tail. Incorrect number of toes. Any apparent weakness in the hind quarters. Any apparent deformity of the spine. Deformity of the skull resulting in an asymmetrical face and/or head.*

*The above listed disqualifications apply to all Persian cats. Additional disqualifications are listed under 'Colors'.

Persian Colors

WHITE: Pure glistening white. *Nose Leather and Paw Pads:* Pink. *Eye Color:* Deep blue or brilliant copper. Odd-eyed whites shall have one blue and one copper eye with equal color depth.

BLACK: Dense coal black, sound from roots to tip of fur. Free from any tinge of rust on tips or smoke undercoat. *Nose Leather:* Black. *Paw Pads:* Black or Brown. *Eye Color:* Brilliant Copper.

BLUE: Blue, lighter shade preferred, one level tone from nose to tip of tail. Sound to the roots. A sound darker shade is more acceptable than an unsound lighter shade. *Nose Leather and Paw Pads:* Blue. *Eye Color:* Brilliant Copper.

RED: Deep, rich, clear, brilliant red; without shading, markings, or ticking. Lips and chin the same color as coat. *Nose Leather and Paw Pads:* Brick Red. *Eye Color:* Brilliant Copper.

CREAM: One level shade of buff cream, without markings. Sound to the roots. Lighter shades preferred. *Nose Leather and Paw Pads:* Pink. *Eye Color:* Brilliant Copper.

CHINCHILLA: Undercoat pure white. Coat on back, flanks, head, and tail sufficiently tipped with black to give the characteristic sparkling silver

Breed Standards

appearance. Legs may be slightly shaded with tipping. Chin and ear tufts, stomach and chest, pure white. Rims of eyes, lips and nose outlined with black. *Nose Leather:* Brick Red. *Paw Pads:* Black. *Eye Color:* Green or Blue-Green. Disqualify for incorrect eye color, incorrect eye color being copper, yellow, gold, amber, or any color other than green or blue-green.

SHADED SILVER: Undercoat white with a mantle of black tipping shading down from sides, face, and tail from dark on the ridge to white on the chin, chest, stomach, and under the tail. Legs to be the same tone as the face. The general effect to be much darker than a chinchilla. Rims of eyes, lips and nose outlined with black. *Nose Leather:* Brick Red. *Paw Pads:* Black. *Eye Color:* Green or Blue-Green. Disqualify for incorrect eye color, incorrect eye color being copper, yellow, gold, amber, or any color other than green or blue-green.

CHINCHILLA GOLDEN: Undercoat rich warm cream. Coat on back, flanks, head, and tail sufficiently tipped with seal brown to give golden appearance. Legs may be slightly shaded with tipping. Chin and ear tufts, stomach and chest, cream. Rims of eyes, lips and nose outlined with seal brown. *Nose Leather:* Deep Rose. *Paw Pads:* Seal Brown. *Eye Color:* Green or Blue-Green. Disqualify for incorrect eye color, incorrect eye color being copper, yellow, gold, amber, or any color other than green or blue-green.

SHADED GOLDEN: Undercoat rich warm cream with a mantle of seal brown tipping shading down from sides, face, and tail from dark on the ridge to cream on the chin, chest, stomach, and under the tail. Legs to be the same tone as the face. The general effect to be much darker than a chinchilla. Rims of eyes, lips, and nose outlined with seal brown. *Nose Leather:* Deep Rose. *Paw Pads:* Seal Brown. *Eye Color:* Green or Blue-Green. Disqualify for incorrect eye color, incorrect eye color being copper, yellow, gold, amber, or any color other than green or blue-green.

Breed Standards

SHELL CAMEO (RED CHINCHILLA): Undercoat white, the coat on the back, flanks, head, and tail to be sufficiently tipped with red to give the characteristic sparkling appearance. Face and legs may be very slightly shaded with tipping. Chin, ear tufts, stomach, and chest white. *Nose Leather and Paw Pads:* Rose. *Eye Color:* Brilliant Copper.

SHADED CAMEO (RED SHADED): Undercoat white with a mantle of red tipping shading down the sides, face, and tail from dark on the ridge to white on the chin, chest, stomach, and under the tail. Legs to be the same tone as face. The general effect to be much redder than the Shell Cameo. *Nose Leather, Rims of Eyes, and Paw Pads:* Rose. *Eye Color:* Brilliant Copper.

SHELL TORTOISESHELL: Undercoat white. Coat on the back, flanks, head, and tail to be delicately tipped in black with well-defined patches of red and cream tipped hairs as in the pattern of the Tortoiseshell. Face and legs may be slightly shaded with tipping. Chin, ear tufts, stomach, and chest white to very slightly tipped. Blaze of red or cream tipping on face is desirable. *Eye Color:* Brilliant Copper.

SHADED TORTOISESHELL: Undercoat white. Mantle of black tipping and clearly defined patches of red and cream tipped hairs as in the pattern of the Tortoiseshell. Shading down the sides, face, and tail from dark on the ridge to slightly tipped or white on the chin, chest, stomach, legs, and under the tail. The general effect is to be much darker than the Shell Tortoiseshell. Blaze of red or cream tipping on the face is desirable. *Eye Color:* Brilliant Copper.

BLACK SMOKE: White undercoat, deeply tipped with black. Cat in repose appears black. In motion the white undercoat is clearly apparent. Points and mask black with narrow band of white at base of hairs next to skin which may be seen only when fur is parted.

Breed Standards

Light silver frill and ear tufts. *Nose Leather and Paw Pads:* Black. *Eye Color:* Brilliant Copper.

BLUE SMOKE: White undercoat, deeply tipped with blue. Cat in repose appears blue. In motion the white undercoat is clearly apparent. Points and mask blue with narrow band of white at base of hairs next to skin which may be seen only when fur is parted. White frill and ear tufts. *Nose Leather and Paw Pads:* Blue. *Eye Color:* Brilliant Copper.

CAMEO SMOKE (RED SMOKE): White undercoat, deeply tipped with red. Cat in repose appears red. In motion the white undercoat is clearly apparent. Points and mask red with narrow band of white at base of hairs next to skin which may be seen only when fur is parted. White frill and ear tufts. *Nose Leather, Rims of Eyes, and Paw Pads:* Rose. *Eye Color:* Brilliant Copper.

SMOKE TORTOISESHELL: White undercoat deeply tipped with black with clearly defined, unbrindled patches of red and cream tipped hairs as in the pattern of the Tortoiseshell. Cat in repose appears Tortoiseshell. In motion the white undercoat is clearly apparent. Face and ears Tortoiseshell pattern with narrow band of white at the base of the hairs next to the skin which may be seen only when fur is parted. White ruff and ear tufts. Blaze of red or cream tipping on face is desirable. *Eye Color:* Brilliant Copper.

BLUE-CREAM SMOKE: White undercoat deeply tipped with blue, with clearly defined patches of cream as in the pattern of the Blue-Cream. Cat in repose appears Blue-Cream. In motion the white undercoat is clearly apparent. Face and ears Blue-Cream pattern with narrow band of white at the base of the hair next to the skin that may be seen only when fur is parted. White ruff and ear tufts. Blaze of cream tipping on face is desirable. *Eye Color:* Brilliant Copper.

CLASSIC TABBY PATTERN: Markings dense, clearly defined,

Breed Standards

and broad. Legs evenly barred with bracelets coming up to meet the body markings. Tail evenly ringed. Several unbroken necklaces on neck and upper chest, the more the better. Frown marks on forehead form intricate letter *M*. Unbroken line runs back from outer corner of eye. Swirls on cheeks. Vertical lines over back of head extend to shoulder markings which are in the shape of a butterfly with both upper and lower wings distinctly outlined and marked with dots inside outline. Back markings consist of a vertical line down the spine from butterfly to tail with a vertical stripe paralleling it on each side, the three stripes well separated by stripes of the ground color. Large solid blotch on each side to be encircled by one or more unbroken rings. Side markings should be the same on both sides. Double vertical row of buttons on chest and stomach.

MACKEREL TABBY PATTERN: Markings dense, clearly defined, and all narrow pencillings. Legs evenly barred with narrow bracelets coming up to meet the body markings. Tail barred. Necklaces on neck and chest distinct, like so many chains. Head barred with an *M* on the forehead. Unbroken lines running back from the eyes. Lines running down the head to meet the shoulders. Spine lines run together to form a narrow saddle. Narrow pencillings run around body.

PATCHED TABBY PATTERN: A Patched Tabby (Torbie) is an established silver, brown, or blue tabby with patches of red and/or cream.

BROWN PATCHED TABBY: Ground color brilliant coppery brown with classic or mackerel tabby markings of dense black with patches of red and/or cream clearly defined on both body and extremities; a blaze of red and/or cream on the face is desirable. Lips and chin the same shade as the rings around the eyes. *Eye Color:* Brilliant Copper.

BLUE PATCHED TABBY: Ground color, including lips and chin, pale bluish ivory with classic or mackerel tabby

Breed Standards

markings of very deep blue affording a good contrast with ground color. Patches of cream clearly defined on both body and extremities; a blaze of cream on the face is desirable. Warm fawn overtones or patina over the whole. *Eye Color:* Brilliant Copper.

SILVER PATCHED TABBY: Ground color, including lips and chin, pale silver with classic or mackerel tabby markings of dense black with patches of red and/or cream clearly defined on both body and extremities. A blaze of red and/or cream on the face is desirable. *Eye Color:* Brilliant Copper or Hazel.

SILVER TABBY: Ground color, including lips and chin, pale, clear silver. Markings dense black. *Nose Leather:* Brick Red. *Paw Pads:* Black. *Eye Color:* Green or Hazel.

RED TABBY: Ground color red. Markings deep, rich red. Lips and chin red. *Nose Leather and Paw Pads:* Brick Red. *Eye Color:* Brilliant Copper.

BROWN TABBY: Ground color brilliant coppery brown. Markings dense black. Lips and chin the same shade as the rings around the eyes. Back of leg black from paw to heel. *Nose Leather:* Brick Red. *Paw Pads:* Black or Brown. *Eye Color:* Brilliant Copper.

BLUE TABBY: Ground color, including lips and chin, pale bluish ivory. Markings a very deep blue affording a good contrast with ground color. Warm fawn overtones or patina over the whole. *Nose Leather:* Old Rose. *Paw Pads:* Rose. *Eye Color:* Brilliant Copper.

CREAM TABBY: Ground color, including lips and chin, very pale cream. Markings of buff or cream sufficiently darker than the ground color to afford good contrast but remaining within the dilute color range. *Nose Leather and Paw Pads:* Pink. *Eye Color:* Brilliant Copper.

CAMEO TABBY: Ground color off-white. Markings red. *Nose Leather and Paw Pads:* Rose. *Eye Color:* Brilliant Copper.

Breed Standards

TORTOISESHELL: Black with unbrindled patches of red and cream. Patches clearly defined and well broken on both body and extremities. Blaze of red or cream on face is desirable. *Eye Color:* Brilliant Copper.

CALICO: White with unbrindled patches of black and red. White predominant on underparts. *Eye Color:* Brilliant Copper.

DILUTE CALICO: White with unbrindled patches of blue and cream. White predominant on underparts. *Eye Color:* Brilliant Copper.

BLUE-CREAM: Blue with patches of solid cream. Patches clearly defined and well broken on both body and extremities. *Eye Color:* Brilliant Copper.

BI-COLOR: Black and white, blue and white, red and white, or cream and white. White feet, legs, undersides, chest, and muzzle. Inverted *V* blaze on face desirable. White under tail and white collar allowable. *Eye Color:* Brilliant Copper.

PERSIAN VAN BI-COLOR: Black and white, red and white, blue and white, or cream and white. White cat with color confined to the extremities; head, tail, and legs. One or two small colored patches on body allowable.

PEKE-FACE RED and PEKE-FACE RED TABBY: The Peke-Face cat should conform in color, markings, and general type to the standards set forth for the red and red tabby Persian cat. The head should resemble as much as possible that of the Pekingese dog from which it gets its name. Nose should be very short and depressed, or indented between the eyes. There should be a decidedly wrinkled muzzle. Eyes round, large, and full, set wide apart, prominent and brilliant.

PERSIAN VAN CALICO: White cat with unbrindled patches of black and red confined to the extremities; head, tail, and legs. One or two small colored patches on body allowable.

PERSIAN VAN DILUTE CALICO: White cat with

Breed Standards

unbrindled patches of blue and cream confined to the extremities; head, tail, and legs. One or two small colored patches on body allowable.

(Note: Cats having more than two small body spots should be shown in the regular Bi-Color Class.)

Allowable outcross breeds - None.

SOMALI

Point Score

HEAD (25)
- Skull................... 6
- Muzzle.................. 6
- Ears 7
- Eye Shape............... 6

BODY (25)
- Torso................... 10
- Legs and Feet........... 10
- Tail.................... 5

COAT (25)
- Texture................. 10
- Length.................. 15

COLOR (25)
- Color................... 10
- Ticking................. 10
- Eye Color............... 5

GENERAL: The overall impression of the Somali is that of a well-proportioned medium to large cat, firm muscular development, lithe, showing an alert, lively interest in all surroundings, with an even disposition and easy to handle. The cat is to give the appearance of activity, sound health, and general vigor.

HEAD: A modified, slightly rounded wedge without flat planes; the brow, cheek, and profile lines all showing a gentle contour. A slight rise from the bridge of the nose to the forehead, which should be of good size with width between the ears flowing into the arched neck without a break.

MUZZLE: Shall follow gentle contours in conformity with the skull, as viewed from the front profile. Chin shall be full, neither undershot nor overshot, having a rounded appearance. The muzzle shall not be sharply

Breed Standards

pointed and there shall be no evidence of snipiness, foxiness, or whisker pinch. Allowance to be made for jowls in adult males.

EARS: Large, alert, moderately pointed, broad, and cupped at the base. Ear set on a line towards the rear of the skull. The inner ear shall have horizontal tufts that reach nearly to the other side of the ear; tufts desirable.

EYES: Almond shaped, large, brilliant, and expressive. Skull aperture neither round nor Oriental. Eyes accented by dark lidskin encircled by light colored area. Above each a short dark vertical pencil stroke with a dark pencil line continuing from the upper lid towards the ear.

BODY: Torso medium long, lithe, and graceful, showing well-developed muscular strength. Rib cage is rounded; back is slightly arched giving the appearance of a cat about to spring; flank level with no tuck up. Conformation strikes a medium between the extremes of cobby and svelte lengthy types.

LEGS AND FEET: Legs in proportion to torso; feet oval and compact. When standing, the Somali gives the impression of being nimble and quick. Toes, five in front and four in back.

TAIL: having a full brush, thick at the base, and slightly tapering. Length in balance with torso.

COAT: Texture very soft to the touch, extremely fine and double coated. The more dense the coat, the better. Length—a medium length coat, except over shoulders, where a slightly shorter length is permitted. Preference is to be given to a cat with ruff and breeches, giving a full-coated appearance to the cat.

PENALIZE: Color faults—cold grey or sandy tone to coat color; mottling or speckling on unticked areas. Pattern faults—necklaces, leg bars, tabby stripes, or bars on body; lack of desired markings on head and tail. Black roots on body.

DISQUALIFY: White locket or groin spot or white anywhere on body other than on the upper

Breed Standards

throat, chin, or nostrils. Any skeletal abnormality. Wrong color paw pads or nose leather. Unbroken necklace. Incorrect number of toes. Kinks in tail.

Somali Colors

RUDDY: Overall impression of an orange-brown or ruddy ticked with black. Color has radiant or glowing quality. Darker shading along the spine allowed. Underside of body and inside of legs and chest to be an even ruddy tone, harmonizing with the top coat; without ticking, barring, necklaces, or belly marks. *Nose Leather:* Tile Red. *Paw Pads:* Black or brown with black between toes and extending upward on rear legs. Off-white on upper throat, lips, and nostrils only. Tail continuing the dark spine lined ending at the black at the tip. Complete absence or rings on tail. Preference given to unmarked ruddy color. Ears tipped with black or dark brown. *Eye Color:* Gold or green, the more richness and depth of color the better.

RED: Warm glowing red ticked with chocolate-brown. Deeper shades of red preferred. Ears and tail tipped with chocolate-brown. *Nose Leather:* Rosy pink. *Paw Pads:* Pink with chocolate-brown between toes, extending slightly beyond paws. *Eye Color:* Gold or green, the more richness and depth the better.

(PLEASE NOTE: The Somali is extremely slow in showing mature ticking and allowances should be made for kittens and young cats.)

Allowable outcross breeds - Abyssinian.

TURKISH ANGORA

Point Score

HEAD 35

BODY 30

COLOR 20

COAT 15

Breed Standards

GENERAL: Solid, firm, giving the impression of grace and flowing movement.

HEAD: Size, small to medium. Wedge-shaped. Wide at top. Definite taper toward chin. Allowance to be made for jowls in stud cat.

EARS: Wide at base, long, pointed, and tufted. Set high on the head and erect.

EYES: large, almond shaped. Slanting upwards slightly.

NOSE: Medium long, gentle slope. No "break."

NECK: Slim and graceful, medium length.

CHIN: Gently rounded. Tip to form a perpendicular line with the nose.

JAW: Tapered.

BODY: Small to medium size in female, slightly larger in male. Torso long, graceful, and lithe. Chest, light framed. Rump slightly higher than front. Bone, fine.

LEGS: Long. Hind legs longer than front.

PAWS: Small and round, dainty. Tufts between toes.

TAIL: Long and tapering, wide at base, narrow at end, full. Carried lower than body but not trailing. When moving, relaxed tail is carried horizontally over the body, sometimes almost touching the head.

COAT: Body coat medium-long, long at ruff. Full brush on tail. Silky with a wavy tendency. Wavier on stomach. Very fine and having a silk-like sheen.

BALANCE: Proportionate in all physical aspects with graceful lithe appearance.

DISQUALIFY: Persian body type. Kinked or abnormal tail.

Turkish Angora Colors

WHITE: Pure white, no other coloring. *Nose Leather and Paw*

Breed Standards

Pads: Pink. *Eye Color:* Odd-Eyed, Blue-Eyed, Amber-Eyed.

BLACK: Dense coal black, sound from roots to tip of fur. Free from any tinge of rust on tips or smoke undercoat. *Nose Leather:* Black. *Paw Pads:* Black or Brown. *Eye Color:* Amber.

BLUE: Blue, lighter shade preferred. One level tone from nose to tip of tail. Sound to the roots. A sound darker shade is more acceptable than an unsound lighter shade. *Nose Leather and Paw Pads:* Blue. *Eye Color:* Amber.

CREAM: One level shade of buff cream without markings. Sound to the roots. Lighter shades preferred. *Nose Leather and Paw Pads:* Pink. *Eye Color:* Amber.

RED: Deep, rich, clear, brilliant red; without shading, markings, or ticking. Lips and chin the same color as coat. *Nose Leather and Paw Pads:* Brick Red. *Eye Color:* Amber.

BLACK SMOKE: White undercoat, deeply tipped with black. Cat in repose appears black. In motion the white undercoat is clearly apparent. Points and mask black with narrow band of white at base of hairs next to skin which may be seen only when fur is parted. *Nose Leather and Paw Pads:* Black. *Eye Color:* Amber.

BLUE SMOKE: White undercoat, deeply tipped with blue. Cat in repose appears blue. In motion the white undercoat is clearly apparent. Points and mask blue with narrow band of white at base of hairs next to skin which may be seen only when fur is parted. *Nose Leather and Paw Pads:* Blue. *Eye Color:* Amber.

CLASSIC TABBY PATTERN: Markings dense, clearly defined, and broad. Legs evenly barred with bracelets coming up to meet the body markings. Tail evenly ringed. Several unbroken necklaces on neck and upper chest, the more the better. Frown marks on forehead form intricate letter *M*. Unbroken line runs back from outer corner of eye. Swirls on cheeks. Vertical lines

Breed Standards

over back of head extend to shoulder markings which are in the shape of a butterfly with both upper and lower wings distinctly outlined and marked with dots inside outline. Back markings consist of a vertical line down the spine from butterfly to tail with a vertical stripe paralleling it on each side, the three stripes well separated by stripes of the ground color. Large solid blotch on each side to be encircled by one or more unbroken rings. Side markings should be the same on both sides. Double vertical row of buttons on chest and stomach.

MACKEREL TABBY PATTERN: Markings dense, clearly defined, and all narrow pencillings. Legs evenly barred with narrow bracelets coming up to meet the body markings. Tail barred. Necklaces on neck and chest distinct, like so many chains. Head barred with an *M* on the forehead. Unbroken lines running back from the eyes. Lines running down the head to meet the shoulders. Spine lines run together to form a narrow saddle. Narrow pencillings run around body.

SILVER TABBY: Ground color, including lips and chin, pale clear silver. Markings dense black. *Nose Leather:* Brick Red. *Paw Pads:* Black. *Eye Color:* Green or Hazel.

RED TABBY: Ground color red. Markings deep rich red. Lips and chin red. *Nose Leather and Paw Pads:* Brick Red. *Eye Color:* Amber.

BROWN TABBY: Ground color brilliant coppery brown. Markings dense black. Lips and chin the same shade as the rings around the eyes. Back of leg black from paw to heel. *Nose Leather:* Brick Red. *Paw Pads:* Black or Brown. *Eye Color:* Amber.

BLUE TABBY: Ground color, including lips and chin, pale bluish ivory. Markings a very deep blue affording a good contrast with ground color. Warm fawn overtones or patina over the whole. *Nose Leather:* Old Rose. *Paw Pads:* Rose. *Eye Color:* Amber.

Breed Standards

CREAM TABBY: Ground color, including lips and chin, very pale cream. Markings of buff or cream sufficiently darker than the ground color to afford good contrast but remaining within the dilute color range. *Nose Leather and Paw Pads:* Pink. *Eye Color:* Amber.

TORTOISESHELL: Black with unbrindled patches of red and cream. Patches clearly defined and well broken on both body and extremities. Blaze of red or cream on face is desirable. *Eye Color:* Amber.

CALICO: White with unbrindled patches of black and red. White predominant on underparts. *Eye Color:* Amber.

DILUTE CALICO: White with unbrindled patches of blue and cream. White predominant on underparts. *Eye Color:* Amber.

BLUE-CREAM: Blue with patches of solid cream. Patches clearly defined and well broken on both body and extremities. *Eye Color:* Amber.

BI-COLOR: Black and white, blue and white, red and white, or cream and white. White feet, legs, undersides, chest, and muzzle. Inverted *V* blaze on face desirable. White under tail and white collar allowable. *Eye Color:* Amber.

Allowable outcross breeds - None.

Suggested Reading

Look for other cat books published by T.F.H. These books are recommended for further enjoyment of your longhaired cat.

CAT OWNER'S ENCYCLOPEDIA OF VETERINARY MEDICINE
New Edition—Revised and Expanded
By Joan O. Joshua, F.R.C.V.S.
ISBN 0-87666-852-X
TFH H-985
Contents: The Cat; Pet and Patient. Restraint, Sedation and Anaesthesia. Signs of Health and Disease, Routine Clinical Examination. The Head. The Eyes. The Mouth. The Ears. The Alimentary Tract. Pancreas, Liver, Spleen Including Diaphragm. Cardiovascular System. Urinary Tract. Reproductive System. Herniae. The Skin. The Skeletal System. Nervous System. Disease Due to Infective Agents. Sepsis. The Cat In Quarantine. The Veterinary Surgeon and Cat Shows. Geriatric Care. Some Common Accidents and Injuries Including Poisoning.
Hard cover, 5½ × 8"; 288 pages

ENCYCLOPEDIA OF AMERICAN CAT BREEDS
By Meredith Wilson
ISBN 0-87666-855-4
TFH H-997
Contents: The Breeds: Abyssinian, American Shorthair, American Wirehair, Balinese, Birman, Bombay, British Shorthair, Burmese, Chartreux, Colorpoint Shorthair, Egyptian Mau, Exotic Shorthair, Havana Brown, Himalayan, Japanese Bobtail, Korat, Maine Coon, Manx, Manx Longhair, Oriental Shorthair, Persian, Ragdoll, Rex, Russian Blue, Scottish Fold, Siamese, Somali, Sphynx, Tonkinese, Turkish Angora.
Hard cover, 5½ × 8"; 352 pages 145 black and white photographs, 100 full-color photographs

PERSIAN CATS AND OTHER LONGHAIRS
By Jeanne Ramsdale
ISBN 0-87666-179-7
TFH H-918

Contents: Pedigrees, Names, And Registrations. The World Of Show Cats. Cat Traits And Tricks. The Right Kitten. He, She, Or It. The Mating Game. The Expectant Mother. The Birth Of A Kitten. Bringing Up The Children. Sustaining The Inner Cat. Cat Comforts At Home And Abroad. Necessary Care For Longhairs. In Sickness And In Health. Show Standards For Longhairs. Recognized Colors Of Longhairs. White Persians. Blue Persians. Red Persians. Cream Persians. Silver Persians. The Mosaic Pattern. Peke-Faced Persians. Hybrid Longhairs. Semi-Longhairs.
Hard cover; 5½ × 8½"; 271 pages 147 black and white photos; 22 color photos